HIPPOCRATES
Father of Medicine

For Hildreth

This book was written for those 10 + up. Since age is only a number I thought you might enjoy it.

Hub Goldly

HIPPOCRATES

Father of Medicine

by HERBERT S. GOLDBERG

Authors Choice Press
New York Lincoln Shanghai

HIPPOCRATES
Father of Medicine

Copyright © 1963, 2006.

Authors Choice Press
an imprint of iUniverse, Inc.

iUniverse books may be ordered through booksellers or by contacting:

iUniverse
2021 Pine Lake Road, Suite 100
Lincoln, NE 68512
www.iuniverse.com
1-800-Authors (1-800-288-4677)

FIRST PRINTING

ISBN-13: 978-0-595-38023-7
ISBN-10: 0-595-38023-9

Printed in the United States of America

To Jacquelyn Louise
and Sheryl Nadine

Contents

HIPPOCRATES
Father of Medicine

The Greek physician Hippocrates, according to the best available records, was born in the year 460 B.C. on the island of Cos, which lies in the southeastern corner of the Aegean Sea. His is a name that has come down through history as one of the greatest of early times. Yet, because he lived so long ago, few facts about his life are positively known.

We do know, however, that this Greek genius lived to be over ninety years old. Fortunately for the science of medicine, he was able to work and flourish in a peaceful time. This was the period known as the Golden Age of Pericles. Hippocrates was in good company indeed, for some of his contemporaries included such famous men as Herodotus the historian, Socrates the philosopher, Sophocles the playwright, and Democritus the scientist.

While it is true that little information has survived of Hippocrates' personal life, he did live and work in this Golden Age—about which a surprising amount *is* known. Moreover, Hippocrates lives on today through his teachings and writings—documents that were assembled almost two hundred years after his death. His fame through the ages rests almost as much on his moral standards as on his scientific genius. His many maxims, for example, reveal a man of wit and wisdom: "Art is long, life is short"; "One man's meat is another man's poison"; "Desperate diseases need desperate remedies."

But it is chiefly as a physician that Hippocrates is remembered today. His introduction of a scientific approach to the study and treatment of disease has deservedly earned for him the title of "Father of Medicine." For centuries, his works remained the foundation of practically all medical and biological knowledge. His approach especially to the problems of sickness and disease drove the opening wedge into the wall of fear that cloaked human illnesses.

"No one disease is either more divine or more human than another . . ." wrote Hippocrates, ". . . but all are alike divine, for each has its own nature, and each disease has a natural cause—and without a natural cause none arise."

This conviction helped to stem the tide of early medical ignorance and superstition and belief in the religious causes of disease, and substituted observation and study.

What were the circumstances—historical and geographical—of the nation that gave rise to this remarkable man? What was the world of Hippocrates like? Let us examine first the country and the people of Greece in the Golden Age and before. Perhaps then we shall be better prepared to reconstruct the story of this master physician.

ONE

Greece. Its Islands and People

It is surprising that ancient Greece, which contributed so much to the cultures, religions, and achievements of our modern world, was smaller in size than the state of Ohio. Nevertheless, this tiny area produced some of the greatest works of literature, architecture, and sculpture created in the past two thousand years. By looking into the story of Greece as it existed some four or five hundred years before the birth of Christ, it may be possible to discover what it was that made these people great.

The Land

At the southeastern tip of Europe, separated from Asia by the Aegean Sea, lies the small, mountainous peninsula which is Greece. This land, together with the numerous islands which surround it, is often referred to as the "cradle of civilization." It was in this ancient land that the fine arts made their greatest advance and where medicine, as we shall see, came from the darkness of superstition into the light of science.

The peninsula of Greece is surrounded by the Aegean Sea on the east, the Ionian Sea on the west, and juts into the Mediterranean Sea on the south. On the north, modern-day Greece is bounded by Turkey, Bulgaria, Yugoslavia, and Albania. This entire area is often referred to as the Balkan States.

The climate of this area, particularly near the coast, is mild and very pleasant. This is due mainly to the presence of the sea, which in winter attracts the mild winds from the west and in summer the dry cooling winds of the northeast. Much of the climate is very similar to that of California in the United States. The rains usually come in the winter, and the dry season begins in May and ends in October. It seldom snows or freezes in the valleys of Greece. Yet the mountaintops may be covered with snow even when the olives, oranges, and almonds are growing in the lowlands. This is the climate in Greece today, and it was the climate of Greece in ancient days.

Because the climate of the lowlands near the sea is so mild, the important crops and marketable products are mainly fruits and grains. Since antiquity, more than two thousand years ago, Greece has been known for its grapes, oranges, figs, olives, oats, and barley. The uplands, or mountains, have contributed timber for fuel and pastures for the grazing of sheep, cattle, goats, and pigs. Thus, the highlands contributed meat and milk products to the diet of the Greek, balancing the cereals, fruits, and vegetables which he obtained from the lowlands.

The bulk of the population is in the lowlands of Greece. These people make their living by agriculture and fishing. In ancient times, the total area of fertile, tillable soil in Greece was less than one-fifth of the entire country, and today it is only a little more. Since most of this fertile soil is in the valleys, the people in the mountains have always been moving southward to the lowlands in the hope of obtaining a better life for themselves. This movement of people operates today as it did in antiquity.

These geographical characteristics of Greece are generally common to all the states of the mainland peninsula and to most of the islands of the surrounding shore. As we discuss the important islands, we shall see that each has mountainous highlands and fertile lowlands and therefore is a perfect geographical miniature of the mainland.

The Islands

The islands surrounding the peninsula of Greece were extremely important in ancient times. Travel overland from Europe in the days before roads and highways was extremely hazardous, and thus the islands on the west coast were the main channels of traffic between the European mid-continent and Greece. On the east coast, they served Greece as steppingstones to Asia and its huge trade market. Consequently, the islands of the Ionian, Aegean, and Mediterranean seas were the central points for the exchange of goods between Europe, Asia, and Egypt to the south.

Moreover, during those early days of primitive sailing vessels, it was important to have numerous safe ports so that movement of goods and people could go on unhampered. Indeed, if the islands of the Aegean Sea had not been so plentiful and close together, it is doubtful whether the Mediterranean area would have been the center of world trade as it was some two thousand years ago.

The islands off the west coast of Greece are called the Ionians; they run alongside the coast and most have very fine harbors. There are seven principal Ionian islands. Among the smallest of these is Ithaca. This island has an area of 40 square miles and is famous as the home of Ulysses, one of the great heroes of Greek mythology. The people of Ithaca are mainly fishermen, although there are some farmers who produce grapes and olives.

Moving south along the west coast of Greece, we encounter Zacynthus (Zante), one of the longest of the Ionian Islands. In ancient times, this island was covered with great forests and produced wheat, wines, and livestock. Today, most of the forests have been used for wood and the land is too rocky for much farming. The other important islands of this group are Corcyra (Corfu) and Leucadia (Leukas), which are the closest Greek islands to Italy.

The true realm of Grecian islands is in the Aegean Sea. These islands number well over a thousand, and they are important in history because many noteworthy contributors to world civilization came from them to the Greek mainland. Moreover, the Aegeans were the link from Europe to Asia, and thus the means of exchange of ideas, culture, and goods between the two continents. Since these islands are so numerous, we shall examine only the most important ones in order to understand the historical and geographical background of this area.

In the northeastern Aegean, ten miles from the Asian continent, yet still part of Greece, is Lesbos. This is a rather large, rich island with an area of over 600 square miles and a modern population of over 150,000. Mount Olympus, the legendary home of the Greek gods, is on this island. The soil there is very fertile and fruits, grains, and vegetables are produced. Fishing is an important occupation, as is the mining of metals, marble, and coal. Just below Lesbos is the island of Chios, also a rich island, although much smaller than Lesbos. Its products include cereals, figs, and timber.

Rhodes is the most easterly island in the Aegean Sea and has an area of about 545 square miles. An elevated mountain range runs from north to south, and extensive forests of ancient pines are found there. These forests at one time were very thick, but they were subsequently thinned down by those who did not replant other trees in their place. Rhodes is also blessed with fertile soil and produces varieties of the finest fruits and vegetables. The valleys afford rich pastures, and the plains produce a wide variety of grain.

The largest island belonging to Greece is in the Mediterranean Sea and is called Crete. It is about 3,200 square miles in area and approximately 160 miles long. Two chains of mountain ranges bounded by forests run through the entire length of the island. The climate is mild and as a result the valleys are fertile; olives are the principal source of wealth. In ancient times, more than a million people lived on Crete, but now less than a third that number call this island home. Crete lies almost directly south of the Greek peninsula on the sea route to Egypt. To the east of Crete, the islands of Kasos and Carpathos (Karpathos) point toward Rhodes and the continent of Asia.

For our story of Hippocrates, however, the most important Grecian island of all is Cos, the birthplace of the physician. This island is in the southeastern corner of the Aegean Sea, very close to the Asian mainland and somewhat north of Rhodes. The principal resources of Cos are grapes (for wine), cereals, melons, and other fruits. All of these crops grow well because of the deep underground springs that provide irrigation. Cos is about 30 miles long, but only 3 or 4 miles wide.

Hippocrates apparently remained on the island for his education as a youth, became a physician, and left Cos at about the age of thirty. To this day there exists a huge tree, called the "Tree of Hippocrates," in the market square of the largest city on Cos. It has a circumference of 45 feet, and no one is quite sure how old it is. Legend has it that under this tree the medical students of Hippocrates sat at the feet of their master.

The People

The Greek nation originally seems to have emerged from three separate divisions of people. These were the Dorians, the Ionians, and the Aeolians. Each of these groups came from a different area of the country and had its own customs and representative cities.

The Dorians were distinguished from other Greeks by their language, their avid celebration of festivals, and the forceful way they directed their government. They were a conquering, warlike people and held many populations under their rule. A class of people known as Helots were completely enslaved and bound to the land which they had to farm for their Dorian masters. In addition, they were required to serve as soldiers in wartime. The Perioeci, a higher, land-owning class, were free and were permitted to carry on trades and professions, but they were still "second-class citizens."

The highest class of the Dorian group were called Spartiates. The Spartiates were the only fully qualified citizens of Sparta, the most important Dorian city, and they alone could hold office in the government. Because of the warlike attitude and powerful rule of these people, the Dorian influence spread throughout much of Greece in ancient times, even to the island of Crete which became predominantly Dorian.

The Ionians were people who lived along the seacoast of the Grecian mainland. They were energetic and wealthy, but not warlike as the Dorians were. They had a democratic form of government and were known for their poetry, literature, philosophy, and science. They first appeared along the Ionian Sea, from which their name originated. The best known of the cities of Ionian origin was Athens. Rivalry between the great Ionian city, Athens, and the great Dorian city, Sparta, grew so great it led to war in 431 B.C. This was called the Peloponnesian War because it took place on the southern part of the mainland of Greece, which was called the Peloponnesus.

Athens, like Sparta, was made up of different classes of people. The upper class were the citizens of Athens. They became citizens by inheriting that right from their parents. A first-class citizen of Athens had to have a father and mother who were both full-blooded Athenian citizens. Only the citizen class in Athens could make laws, vote, and direct the government. The next lowest class in Athens at the time were the metics, or foreign born. These were people who were not born in Athens, but had come there from some other part of the country. They were welcome in Athens and could take part in all the activities of the community except the government. Metics were lawyers, teachers, artists, and doctors. Although they might achieve many honors, they could never become equal to the first-class citizens of Athens. The best known of the metics of Athens was Hippocrates of Cos, who left his native island to come to Athens as a young man.

The most unfortunate of the classes of people in ancient Athens were the slaves. They functioned only as servants in their masters' households. They did have a few rights according to law, however. If their master was cruel, they could demand to be sold to a new master—and such a demand was usually granted. Nevertheless, these people were the lowest and most unfortunate class of Athenians.

The third great division of Greek peoples were known as the Aeolians. It is believed that they once lived on the northern mainland of Greece, but were later driven across the Aegean Sea by invading armies. They became scattered all about the islands and the coast of Asia Minor. They spoke their own dialect and settled wherever they could find rich agricultural land. They were not much interested in wars and politics; instead they were devoted to music and song. Indeed, they created new styles of poetry, literature, and music which contributed much to the high culture of the Greeks. The island of Lesbos was the most important of the Aeolian lands.

Growing Up in Ancient Greece

The birth of Hippocrates of Cos took place in 460 B.C. on the 18th day of August. The occasion was celebrated by festivals and feasts, because the birth of a boy was particularly honored in those days of Greece. Gifts were brought by members of the family, relatives, and friends.

As was the custom, the naming of the infant took place on the tenth day after the birth. It was a very common practice at that time to give the first-born boy the name of his grandfather, and so Hippocrates II was named for his grandfather, Hippocrates I. We shall see later how this method of choosing names led to confusion in history. Many medical documents and records have been unearthed which are simply signed Hippocrates, and there is no way of being certain which Hippocrates produced them.

The family of Hippocrates consisted of his mother, Praxithea; his grandmother, Phainarete, wife of his grandfather Hippocrates I; his father, Heracleides; and his brother, Soranus. There were also several other brothers, but their names have been lost to history.

The years of Hippocrates' early childhood were spent in his island home under the care of his mother and his nurse. The nurse was a female slave of the household, carefully selected for her ability to help raise children. She taught Hippocrates to speak correctly and to learn nursery rhymes, fables, and history.

Hippocrates' mother, Praxithea, was usually busy directing the servants, seeing to the preparation of the meals, and running the household. Like all women of the time, she confined most of her activity to being a housewife. Indeed, one of the fundamentals of Greek family life was that the father of the family was the master of the household, while his wife was only to be concerned with raising the children, caring for the home, and nursing the sick. Thus, under the watchful eyes of his mother and his nurse, Hippocrates spent his earliest years in his home and at play with the other young boys of Cos.

Hippocrates lived in a large two-story house made of sun-dried brick; inside, the walls and floors were decorated with designs painted by local artists. His home also had lovely rugs and tapestries, dishes of gold, silver, and bronze, and even cups set with precious jewels.

One of the most pleasant occasions for Hippocrates, as for all young boys today, was mealtime. As in our own times, three meals were eaten during the day. The first was taken upon arising. It was usually very light and consisted of bread and a beverage, most often wine. Coffee, tea, cocoa, and similar drinks were not known at that time. Milk was available from sheep and goats, but it was consumed mostly in the country. Wine, then, often diluted with water, was the staple beverage.

The second meal of the day came just after noon. It was usually a hot cooked meal and corresponded to our lunch.

The principal meal of the day, and the one most enjoyed by all the family, was dinner in the evening. There were usually two courses, the main course and a dessert. Dinner was a time for jokes, songs, storytelling, and general companionship. Meals were usually prepared by the mother; if she was fortunate enough to have maids, they helped. There were no specialized cooks among the servants as are found in some households today.

Dining utensils were very few. There were plates and cups, but no knives or forks. The Greeks ate, for the most part, with their fingers, although soups and gravies were eaten with spoons. There were no napkins or tablecloths. The dining room was equipped with a very low table at which the women and children sat. The men, however, always had a couch. They would lean their left shoulders on cushions and, in this semi-reclined position, consume their meal!

The kinds of food eaten in Hippocrates' day were very much the same as man has eaten since the beginning of time. While various kinds of meat were found at the open-air market—beef, veal, mutton, pork, and lamb—historical records tell us that meat was eaten by the early Greeks only rarely. It was expensive and not as popular as fish. The ancient Greeks also had a large variety of vegetables such as radishes, beans, spinach, peas, and lettuce, but no potatoes or tomatoes. There were many fruits, among them apples, cherries, peaches, pears, plums, figs, grapes, and olives. All these, of course, were abundant because of the warm climate which was ideal for growing these products.

The basic food found at all Greek meals was bread. In the richer homes the bread was made of wheat, purchased from a professional baker in loaves of all sizes and shapes. The poorer homes had to be satisfied with homemade barley or rice cakes.

One custom of the ancient Greeks was to use dinner as occasions for celebrating festivals, holidays, births, and weddings. Whenever these occasions arose, huge banquets, called *symposiums,* were held. During symposiums, Hippocrates and the other children had to join the women in another part of the house, for only men could participate in them. Thus, Hippocrates had to wait until he was a man before he could enjoy these festive gatherings.

The principal garments of the day were the *chiton,* or tunic, the *himation,* a kind of cloak, and sandals. These garments were worn by men, women, and children. The chiton was actually a sleeveless shirt—long and loose fitting—and it varied in weight with the locality, season of the year, and personal taste. Worn next to the skin, it was originally an oblong piece of cloth drawn around the body and caught at the shoulders with fastenings. In shape, style, and color the women's chiton was more elaborate than the men's. By means of silks, linens, and woolens, the women could devise a variety of colorful garments. In addition, jewelry was worn to adorn the clothes. The outer garment was the mantle or himation. It was a rectangular piece of cloth considerably longer than the chiton. While both sexes wore this, the women's were decorated by embroidery and tassels. The himation was worn over the chiton.

Hippocrates wore these garments throughout his life. He never wore trousers, for they were unknown to the Greeks, although Persians were known to use them. As a young man, Hippocrates also wore a garment called a *chlamys,* a specialized type of mantle—a square-cut cape that flowed over the shoulders—worn by all youths of the period.

Footwear in Greece usually consisted of simple sandals, although there is evidence that slippers, boots, and shoes were also worn. Foot covering was only worn outdoors, since Greek men and women went barefoot in the home.

The final article of clothing occasionally worn by Greeks was some form of headdress, although only for special occasions such as a long journey or bad weather. Men wore wide-brimmed hats of wool with low crowns. Women occasionally wore veils of linen which covered the head and face. Workmen often wore wool caps to keep dust and dirt from the hair. In general, however, the ancient Greeks went bareheaded because of sunny, temperate climate.

Two thousand years ago in Greece, young children were as interested in toys and games as they are today.

Historical records show that Hippocrates as a boy had his choice of tops, balls, yo-yos, and toy animals to play with. Most children also had pets as they do today, dogs and cats being the favorites.

Hippocrates also took part in a number of games which were played by boys and girls of the time. Many of these are known to us today. For example, Hippocrates played handball, hide-and-seek, tug-of-war, leap-frog, and blindman's buff. Greek boys also played a popular game called *ostracinda*. The boys lined up in two groups, one on either side of a mark drawn on the ground. One boy took a piece from a broken pot, white on one face and black on the other, and tossed it into the air, shouting, "Night or day." The white face belonged to one side, the black face to the other. If it chanced to fall black face up, the boys on the black side ran, and those on the other side gave chase. When all the boys on one side were caught and held prisoner, they lost the game.

At the age of seven, Hippocrates left the charge of his nurse and was placed under the care of a man-servant. This did not happen with girls, who always remained with their nurses and were trained early for household duties. Hippocrates as a young boy, however, went under the direction of an elderly man of the household to begin his training for the outside world. It was the duty of the manservant to take Hippocrates to primary school, carry his books and supplies, and bring him home again.

The Early Education of Hippocrates

Promptly at the age of seven, Hippocrates joined the boys of similar age in his neighborhood and went to primary school. He would remain there for the next nine years.

The *curriculum,* or course of study, was divided into two parts—physical education and mental discipline. Mental discipline meant learning how to read, write, and spell. Reading was always done aloud in order to learn correct enunciation and clear expression. Writing exercises were done with a pen on papyrus, the first form of paper (discovered by the Egyptians). Hippocrates was also required to study music, singing, poetry, and to learn to play the flute and the lyre, a small harp-like instrument.

Such schooling as this was obviously not intended to teach a trade or to help the student learn a profession. The purpose of formal schooling in ancient Greece was to produce cultured gentlemen who were trained for citizenship and leadership. As we shall see later, training for the trades and professions was learned by the apprentice system in shops and offices.

The teachers in the Greek schools were men of education and culture who were not wealthy and who used their knowledge to earn a living. In the higher grades, such as the equivalent of our high school or college, the teachers were mostly respected philosophers who refused to take money for their work as teachers of truth.

Once a youth entered school, he soon learned that the teacher's authority was absolute. No one was permitted to enter the classroom during school hours. The teacher could administer discipline by any method he chose, including the strap.

In Greece, schooling was required of all boys between the ages of seven and sixteen. At the end of this period, poor boys left school to go to work, while the sons of wealthy parents went on to the higher schools taught by the philosophers.

Those who did not enter the higher philosophical schools could still go to institutions devoted to athletic training. These were called *gymnasiums;* in them, students received instructions in sports and bodily development, as well as in music, literature, and oratory. Every city in ancient Greece had at least one gymnasium. The most famous of these were the Academy and the Lyceum, both in Athens.

The gymnasium had dressing rooms, a 200-yard race course, a course for spear and discus throwing, shower and swimming rooms, and space for horseback riding. Also in the gymnasium was the *palaestra,* or wrestling school. Here boys trained for wrestling, boxing, jumping, and the like.

From the time he was sixteen until he was eighteen, Hippocrates attended the gymnasium in Cos. Here he was put through the vigorous curriculum of physical training and athletics. The athletic contests were many and varied, including broad jumping, boxing, and sprinting. Perhaps the most colorful and exciting of all contests was the torch race. This was run by a team of as many as ten, in relays, carrying a lighted torch. Sometimes these torch races were on horseback. Another sport originating in ancient Greece and widely practiced by youths of Hippocrates' time was discus throwing. In those days, the discus was made of bronze and weighed almost ten pounds. At modern olympic games, however, the discus is made of wood and brass and weighs less than five pounds.

Another throwing game at the gymnasium involved

27

hurling the spear for distance and accuracy. The spear was about six feet long, and it was the same weapon that was used in time of war against the enemies of Greece. Thus, the training of the youth had an important role in wartime as well as peace. For example, one racing event consisted of men dressed in full armor running over a course of 400 yards. This was a military exercise more than a sport and was highly popular.

Yet another popular sport of the gymnasium was boxing, but it was conducted much differently than it is today. There were no ring enclosures and no rounds limiting the time. Opponents simply fought to the finish. Most surprising of all, there were no weight divisions. This meant a lightweight could draw a heavyweight as an opponent. The boxers wore no gloves, simply a leather thong strapped around their fists.

When the boys were eighteen, their education was considered completed in all its general aspects. This was the time when a young man could choose to learn a profession or go into agriculture, business, or politics. All of these fields were to be learned by the apprentice method—on the job. Oftentimes, however, there was one factor that intervened. The first duty of each male citizen of ancient Greece, particularly if he lived in Athens, was to serve two years in the army. Hippocrates, who happened to reside on the isle of Cos, was not required to enter the army and thus was able to begin his study of medicine.

The young man began his study of medicine under the direction of his father, Heracleides, who was a descendant of a group of priest-physicians known as *Asclepiads*. This name came from the first important physician of the early Greek people, Asclepius, who was worshiped as the god of healing. Thus, it is apparent that long before Hippocrates came on the scene, medicine was very closely related to religion and superstition. The followers of Asclepius, calling themselves Asclepiads, worshiped in healing temples called *Asclepieions*. Hence, the Asclepiads can be looked upon as an ancient medical guild of which Hippocrates, because of his having been born the son of one of these physicians, was a member.

At this time—it was the fifth century before the Christian era—there were three Asclepiad medical schools. They were not medical schools as we know them today, of course, but rather centers of medical teaching, usually located in the healing temples. The three schools were on the island of Rhodes, the island of Cos, and at Cnidus, which juts out from the coast of Asia Minor into the Aegean Sea between Cos and Rhodes.

The medical school located on the island of Rhodes was not very prominent and few historical reports are available about it. The two remaining medical learning centers at Cos and Cnidus were, however, very prominent. The teachers in each of these schools belonged to the family of Asclepiads which claimed direct descent from Asclepius himself. The students were either sons of Asclepiads or apprentices who paid fees to be admitted to the family, and who were to be taught the theory and practice of medicine.

Actually, there was no prescribed course of study. A student attached himself to a physician and served as his assistant; he also lived, ate, and slept with his teacher. As the student accompanied the doctor on his cases, treated patients, received instructions, and studied the medical literature, he himself eventually became skilled at medicine. In this way, the medical student of ancient Greece secured his education in medicine. And Hippocrates, according to this tradition, studied medicine under the guidance of his father, Heracleides. In addition to his studies at Cos, Hippocrates made frequent voyages for the purpose of further study to the islands of the Aegean Sea, the mainland of Greece, and even to Egypt and Libya. Wherever he went, he studied the medical traditions of the locality, treated patients, and increased his knowledge of medicine. After the death of his father, Hippocrates, as his medical reputation spread, was to become the master physician of the *Coans,* or adherents of the Cos School.

The chief physician of the Cnidian School at this time was a man named Euryphon. He was somewhat older than Hippocrates and led his school in opposition to the school of Cos. Thus, a traditional rivalry developed between the Asclepiads of Cos and Cnidus. The medical school at Cnidus reflected the influence of Egyptian culture. Euryphon wrote a series of medical prescriptions called the *Cnidian Maxims.* Although these were very important to practical medicine, they were not as important or useful as Hippocrates' later writings. The school at Cnidus was criticized by the Coans for spending too much time on classification of diseases and not enough on viewing or treating the patient as a whole person. In addition, the Cnidian School recommended treatments that were directed to the restoration of physical harmony; they relied on changes of diet—accompanied by friction—bathing, and exercise. Hippocrates, on the other hand, felt that remedies should be more concerned with the well-being of the patient's mind as well as his body.

Thus, the medicine taught at the school of Cos was founded much more on concern for the patient than concern for the disease. Its members paid more attention to objective symptoms and did not rely too heavily upon the statements of the patient. Employing their special senses to the limit when examining a patient, they did not concern themselves with theories. Moreover, they recognized the systemic nature of disease; that is, they held that disease was generally not limited to a certain part of the body, although it might be most pronounced in one organ of the body. In particular, the Coans studied *acute diseases*—those attended with symptoms of some severity and coming rapidly to a crisis.

While this group attempted, as far as possible, to start with individual observation, the Cnidian School was concerned chiefly with knowledge derived from the mysteries. It developed directly, in continuous tradition, from archaic Greek, Babylonian, and Egyptian healing, so that the Cnidian School worked largely in a deductive manner.

Although he is primarily known today as a physician, we know that Hippocrates was also a remarkable teacher. At the height of his fame, he gathered students from all over the ancient world who were attracted by his reputation. Legend has it that many, many students sat at his feet under the so-called "Tree of Hippocrates" and were thus indoctrinated into medicine.

In his writings, Hippocrates described those characteristics that were most desirable for a student of medicine. He wrote that for a man to be truly suited to the practice of medicine, he must have an instinctive liking for it, the necessary training and education, and the time and industriousness to undertake it. Hippocrates particularly stressed the requisite of a natural liking for medicine, since a reluctant student seldom does well. On the other hand, instruction in the science is easy when the student has a natural desire to learn about it. Furthermore, long-term study on the part of the student is necessary according to Hippocrates, if instruction, firmly planted in his mind, is to bring forth good and fruitful knowledge.

To fully understand the status of the physician at this time in ancient Greece, a look at the learned professions of the day is in order. In this way it can be seen what professions and skills were available to a young man about to embark on a career.

The Learned Professions and the Trades
in Hippocrates' Time

The professions practiced in Greece during Hippocrates' era were very similar to those practiced today. There were lawyers, doctors, professors, sculptors, musicians, artists, and writers. These were primarily the professions which required education and talent acquired over long years. Those who entered them usually came from wealthy homes, and could thus afford the cost and leisure of learning these professions.

Of equal importance to the daily life of the ancient Greeks were the tradesmen. These included farmers, carpenters, blacksmiths, jewelers, cooks, bakers, shoemakers, and miners, among many others.

As we examine some of the trades and professions of Hippocrates' Greece, we can compare the status of the medical profession as it stood more than two thousand years ago with that of other occupations.

Law

Every Greek citizen who had business before courts was expected to represent himself. If he did not know the law or could not prepare his speech, he employed a person who was versed in the subject and whose profession it was to write legal speeches. Such a person was called a "logographer."

When public affairs were at stake or international problems were to be debated, the state employed an advocate to present its cause and defend its interest. However, since study of law was required of all good citizens, it did not serve as an especially great attraction for a youth seeking a career.

Publishing

There were publishers in Greece to supply the reading public's thirst for knowledge, to supply the schools with necessary texts, and to export books to foreign countries. The publisher or the author of a book took all the chances of gain or loss.

In order to make many duplicates of books, copyists were employed. One person read the material very slowly, then others copied it as rapidly and as accurately as they could.

During the classical Greek period, no punctuation or paragraphing was used; this was not introduced until later. The letters were all in capitals and words were not even separated.

Booksellers

In ancient Greece, there were individual booksellers, rather than the bookstores we have today. Some of the booksellers specialized in autographed copies, for which they asked an enormous price. Many of them had forged copies. Instead of modern book advertising methods using show windows, television, newspapers, and magazines, the ancient booksellers advertised their wares by reading aloud from some of the works.

Art and Sculpture

The Greeks had a great love of beauty. So successful were their efforts in creating it that their temples, statues, and painting have been admired and imitated ever since. Even their cooking utensils, such as pots and pans, mixing bowls, drinking cups, were molded

37

into shapes of exquisite perfection and were painted with rare grace and charm. Indeed, it has been said that the Greeks could not have made anything ugly if they had tried!

Until the time of the Peloponnesian War (413–404 B.C.), artists were supported by the state and obtained fees from it. After that time, artists and sculptors were dependent upon private support.

The greatest sculptor of the fifth century was Phidias, whose still-surviving masterpiece is the gold and ivory statue of Zeus, ruler of the Olympian gods.

The Medical Profession

In classical Greece, the profession dealing with medicine and surgery was very highly respected. Doctors, in fact, were looked upon as descendants of the healing god, Apollo. They were highly esteemed for this reason.

As we have seen, a young man who wished to become a doctor was usually apprenticed to a general practitioner. Instruction was personal and individual. More often than not, physicians' sons would take up the same profession as their fathers. Any man who became sufficiently trained and qualified was free to "hang out his shingle" as a doctor in ancient Greece. However, no woman could be recognized as a physician, either by the profession or by the public.

There were physicians recognized by the state and actually employed by the state, not only at the well-known health treatment centers of Cos and Athens, but also in general practice. These doctors, under the direction of the state authorities, provided free treatment for the poor of the city and even for strangers visiting there. In addition, it was the duty of such subsidized doctors to care for the public health, to fight epidemics, and to give instruction in dietetics and hygiene. The state also, as a matter of course, employed physicians and surgeons for service in the army and navy. The selection of all such salaried doctors depended upon their training and their success in private practice. They were well rewarded for their services.

In private practice, the Greek doctor was paid fees by his patients. It is also clear from contemporary writings that the Greek doctor, like his modern successor, did charity work. Fees varied in ancient times according to the ability of the patient to pay.

Unfortunately, in addition to the reputable doctors there were, in ancient Greece, many quacks and fakers who palmed off their services on the ignorant. These charlatans, borrowing the idea from the sacred serpents in the temples of Asclepius, sometimes carried snakes with them to impress the unsuspecting with their super-human skill.

The ancient Greek general practitioner, like his modern counterpart, usually divided his activities between office practice and house visits. His office, the sign of which was likely to be a statue of Asclepius, was a small duplicate of the great healing temple. It was provided with baths of various types, with all the drugs and other paraphernalia of the pharmacy, together with surgical instruments in great variety—most of which could be duplicated in a modern surgeon's instrument cabinet. For the Greek doctor was always both physician and surgeon, as well as pharmacist. Moreover, like the modern practitioner, the busy doctor of ancient times also would turn over to an assistant or to a disciple his simpler cases and much of his routine practice.

As for dentistry, if we may judge by the skulls in museums, the Greeks did not have much need of the dentist's services; their teeth were, for the most part, remarkably well preserved.

Specialization came late in the history of Greek medicine. Eye specialists, specialists in women's diseases, and dentists began to appear, although the general practitioner continued to combine the skills of physician, surgeon, oculist, gynecologist, podiatrist, and dentist.

Together with the physicians, there is evidence of the existence in Greece of others who were concerned with health. Physicians ordinarily prepared medicine themselves, but sometimes they also had them prepared by a *rhizotomist* (meaning a root cutter) who was regarded as the assistant of the physician. The rhizotomist collected the roots and prepared them after drying and grinding. Later the rhizotomists became pharmacists and also prepared other drugs.

Medical skill and training in Greece advanced with more rapid strides than did sanitation and hygiene. Nevertheless, the ancient Greek authors had much to say about health and order. Disease, according to Plato, was a lack of adjustment, a "disharmony." True, their athletic training and frequent bathing contributed much to their physical fitness; however, had Greece not been a land of sunshine and fresh air, the people could hardly have survived. Even Athens had no adequate system of sewers or of water supply; its streets were not clean. Epidemics were frequent and infant mortality ran high. There was a very real need for trained doctors, but they were not always summoned when needed.

The Greek housewife was responsible for the health of the household; and, since she was expected to exercise every possible economy, she often avoided doctor's bills by resorting to her own preparations, charms and spells, amulets, and magic. To assist at the birth of her children she called in not a doctor but a midwife.

Labor and Trades

In ancient Greece, there was an aristocracy of wealthy and independent artists and craftsmen who served the state and who were above accepting pay for their work. At all times, however, there were also the "common laborers and tradesmen" who depended upon the work of their hands for their daily bread.

The Greek gentleman felt that any work accompanied by dirt or discomfort, any labor that interfered with dignity or beauty or with the attainment of "excellence" of body or mind, was to be avoided as unbecoming a gentleman. For this work, there was the laborer and tradesman.

Most of the necessary products in Greece were either produced in the home itself or supplied by artisans working in small shops. The bulk of the clothing was made from homespun wool or flax. True, there were tailors in Greece, but only the wealthy could afford them. Very satisfactory clothing could be made in the home, for the simple tunics and mantles required no tailoring, no elaborate cutting and fitting. The hats worn by travelers, hunters, artisans, and slaves had to be purchased from a hatter. Shoes were usually not made in the home. If a person needed new footwear, he would go to a cobbler's shop.

Trades and crafts were many and varied. There were farmers, gardeners, porters, carpenters, architects, cabinetmakers, painters, sculptors, stonemasons, potters, blacksmiths, cutlers, goldsmiths and jewelers, miners, millers, cooks and confectioners, tanners, weavers, tailors, dyers, barbers, an array of market people, and a host of artisans.

Carpenters

The Greek carpenter not only installed all the woodwork called for in building a house, he also made all sorts of household furniture, farm implements, and wooden tools for trades and crafts. Many of the tools used then could easily be found in a modern-day carpenter's tool chest.

Barbers

Greek gentlemen were very conscious of their personal appearance. As a result, barbering was an important trade in ancient Greece and barbers were extensively patronized. In fact, the shops became clubrooms where men gathered not only for service but for the latest news, ideas, and gossip.

The barber not only shaved and cut the hair of his patrons, he would also curl their hair and beards and manicure their hands and feet. He also did minor surgical operations such as bleeding, and removing warts. In addition, the Greek barber was a specialist in perfumes, ointments, hair dyes, hair restorers, and cosmetics of every kind.

F I V E

Medicine Before Hippocrates

Historical facts of antiquity are gathered from written records in the form of inscriptions on clay tablets, stone, and other writing surfaces. Prehistorical events are discovered from unearthed flints, shards, bones, horns, teeth, or houses.

But information about medicine in ancient times is learned from carvings, paintings in caves, and engravings on stones. Moreover, we have some evidence of disease yielded by fossilized human and animal remains. The reason that so little written information is left concerning prehistorical medicine is that no one bothered to record much of what was observed. Actually, written medical information didn't get its real start until shortly before the time of Hippocrates.

We do know, however, that the practice of medicine in early times was extremely elementary. This was necessarily so because at the dawn of human history, man's food and habits were far simpler and more in harmony with nature than they are in our complicated modern society.

Early Medical Procedures

The methods of "operating" on a skull injury in prehistorical times included drilling, scraping, cutting, and sawing. The "instruments" employed were made of flint, stone, or fragments of shell. The purpose of such operations was to afford relief from convulsions, epilepsy, headache, and mental disorders. But an operation on a person's skull in primitive times was not so much to affect the cranial contents or even the skull itself, but rather to afford an opening for the evil spirit to escape from the head of the sufferer.

On the walls of the caves of ancient France and Spain (7000 B.C.), drawings and silhouettes of operations on legs, arms, and fingers can be seen. Some are clearly amputations. The need for amputation might have suggested itself to the prehistorical surgeon because of the following reasons: (1) realization that hopeless damage had been done to the parts; (2) knowledge of the potentially fatal effect of snakebite; (3) for ceremonial and sacrificial reasons; and (4) realization

46

that a person with a badly injured organ might be better off if it were removed.

The term "medicine man," as applied to primitive healers, has no connection with a knowledge of medicine, pharmacy, or even surgery. It is associated with appeasing the spirits. When the medicine man amputated a finger or opened a vein for bloodletting, he did so without any intention of counteracting a disease condition. His purpose was to permit the exit of an evil spirit from the body, and for this purpose alone he employed a surgical procedure. Indeed, both medicine and surgery appear to have had their beginnings in magic.

Egyptian Medicine

Egyptian papyri reveal that as early as 3500 B.C. the people of the Nile possessed a well-grounded knowledge of the art of medicine. They thought of the heart as the center of action during life, and they knew it ceased to be active immediately upon death. Through the precise study of mummies, much has been learned about Egyptian medicine.

In Egyptian mythology, the gods concerned with health held an important place; in fact, the control of health was attributed more or less to all of the gods. Egyptian medicine was predominantly mystical and was conducted by priests in those times. In addition, Oriental medical influences prevailed in Egypt, since it had frequent contact with the East.

Certain remedies and prescriptions which are known to have been frequently used by the Egyptians were: honey, beer, yeast, oil, dates, figs, onions, garlic, and flaxseed. Other medicines often prescribed were lettuce, crocus, opium, and even parts of animals such as the fat, the brain, and the blood.

In the Ebers Papyrus, which contains some of the first written medical records, one example of a medical prescription by a physician is:

If you examine a person who suffers from pains in the stomach and is sick in the arms and the stomach, and it appears that it is the disease, uat, you will say: "Death has entered into the mouth and has taken its seat there": you will prepare a remedy composed of the following plants: The stalks of the plant tehua, mint, the red seeds of the plant sechet; and you will have them cooked in beer; you will give it to the sick person to drink, then you will put your hands on the sick person and his arm will be easily extended without pain, and then you will say: "The disease has gone out from the intestine, it is not necessary to repeat the medicine."

Thus, the physician's profession in early Egypt was, as it still is today among many peoples, intimately bound up with religion. The first doctor of whom records are available was a priest and many of the functions of the priest were magical in character. The common therapeutical methods—that is, healing or curing diseased persons—were prayers by which demons were expelled. Frequently, their expulsion was effected by words and gestures. Often such rites included a strange mixture of drink and some mystic words to recite. The concoction was intended, not to counteract the condition of the patient, but to disgust the demon who had taken possession of the patient so that he would voluntarily leave the victim.

Chinese Medicine

According to ancient legends, Chinese medicine began during the reign of Emperor Shen Nung, who is said to have lived about 2700 B.C.

In ancient China, the practice of medicine swarmed with countless good and evil spirits. The good ones, the Chinese believed, moved through the air in a curve; the bad ones in a straight line. This fantastic belief influenced the development of Chinese architecture. The roofs of houses, pagodas, gateways, and all other conspicuous structures are curved. Due also to this belief, there are no straight highways in China, and even the development of straight railways has been hindered.

The Chinese physician attributed no importance to the history of the patient and made his diagnosis without consulting it. The better-class physicians would inquire about the patient's family history and present condition, inspect the body, but not the excreta, and listen to voice changes.

Among the most frequent diseases in China is smallpox, of which there have been great epidemics. Inoculation against smallpox was known from ancient times. The crust of a pustule was pulverized and introduced into the nose or was insufflated with a bamboo tube; for boys, the inoculation was made in the left nostril and for girls, in the right nostril.

Together with the gradual penetration of foreign missionaries into China throughout the nineteenth century, European and American hospitals and medical schools were established, which have slowly taught scientific medicine to Chinese students and accustomed the people to the new methods. Today almost every Chinese province has its modern hospital.

Japanese Medicine

The influence of Chinese medicine was early extended to Japan. With the arrival of the Portuguese in 1542, European medical practice and methods began to penetrate that country. Later, a group of Dutch physicians brought to Japan the teachings of the great Flemish physicians. The first period of Japanese medicine was exclusively magic. The second was called *Yeddo,* during which European medicine penetrated slowly into the Japanese schools. Medical science and practice in Japan have made great advances in the present century, and today compare favorably with those of world leaders.

Hebrew Medicine

In the Biblical concept of medicine the priests, who had the high function of supervising all religious ceremonies and acting as interpreters of the divine will, were the only ones to whom the practice of medicine was officially allocated. The art of healing was reserved for the one God, and the priests were the interpreters and fulfillers of His laws and His will. Thus the people of Israel had their priest-physicians.

Among the most frequently occurring diseases in Biblical times were leprosy, dysentery, and mental diseases. At this period, too, the origin of a particular epidemic was sometimes attributed to the most unusual causes; for example, the census-taking was thought to be a cause of epidemics.

A very important part of treating disease was given over to ritual ceremonies—it being granted that to some people supernatural powers were accorded. For example, a man of God was supposed to have the power to transfer leprosy from one person to another. Using a number of charms, a priest could "dry up the thigh and swell the stomach" of a wrongdoer by making him drink water in which had been immersed a curse written on parchment. Remedies were essentially divine or magical. Using magic, one could obtain the resurrection of the dead, as is told by the prophet Elijah. Elijah allegedly brought a child back to life by blowing into its mouth, employing a rite similar to a Babylonian practice.

Thus, the major contribution of the Jewish people to medicine originated in their religious rituals and the

Mosaic laws. In their strict regulations concerning dietary laws, cleanliness, methods of slaughter of animals, and health guides, the Mosaic laws really established the basis for public health medicine which today is part of every municipal public health code.

The Greek Asclepieia

As has been indicated earlier, the status of medicine when Hippocrates was a boy was high, although it was not very scientific. The physicians were primarily of the cult of Asclepius and they practiced their art in healing temples called Asclepieia. Here is essentially what happened to a patient in ancient Greece some two thousand years ago when he went to the temple to be healed:

Before he could enter the temple, the patient was first prepared by a strict fasting. Without such a purifying ritual, no person might be admitted to the temple.

Once inside, the patient would be met by the priest. He would then be told stories of previous cures effected by the god and, in general, everything was done to convince the patient that he would recover. Prayer and some form of ceremonial purification by washing were followed by an offering to the god. This was most often

53

a cock, occasionally a ram or an ox, according to the means of the patient. This might be placed on the altar by the supplicant, but in some cases, at least, it was given to an attendant whose duty it was to determine whether the offering was acceptable.

If it was, the patient entered upon the first stage of the cure. This, known as the ceremony of "lying-in" or "temple-sleep," was the most impressive part of the ritual. The patients lay side by side in a long open-air portico covered at the top and open at the side. Lights were put out by the attendants and all were told to go to sleep. Occasionally hypnotic drugs were administered.

Here the sufferers spent the night, and during sleep dreams were supposed to come to them in which they were cured, or in which a means of cure was revealed. During the night, tame snakes, or in some instances dogs, were allowed access to the temple. Contact with the animal, which licked sore places or blind eyes, was believed to aid in the cure. In many instances, a cure actually did follow, indicating that the will of the god had been obeyed. If no cure ensued, it meant that the patient had neglected to do something that he should have done.

In the event of a cure, it was the custom to consecrate an offering to the god or present a model of the diseased

54

part of the body—made perhaps of gold or silver—which could be hung up in the temple.

During their stay in the Asclepieion, the patients received a varying amount of medical attention, chiefly of a general hygienic nature. The mystic rituals, however, were not the same in all temples; the relative proportion of medicine to magic depended upon the views of the Asclepiads in each shrine. Yet it is apparent that the Asclepiads must have possessed a good working knowledge not only of the symptomatology of disease, but also of prognosis. They were, in fact, resident physicians with a good opportunity for observation. They also had access to libraries of case records.

Interestingly enough, birth and death were not permitted in the Asclepieia. Hence, it was necessary for the attendants to recognize when a case was at death's door so that admission could be refused.

This, then, was the status of medicine in Greece immediately before Hippocrates came on the scene. As we shall see, Hippocrates had to overcome this ritualistic, magical type of medicine in order to develop his scientific form of medicine. In the next pages, we shall see what scientific changes Hippocrates brought about, and how they affected his relationship with patients on a day-to-day basis.

Medicine Becomes a Science

Modern medicine is divided into a great number of different fields and special branches. These include anatomy, physiology, psychiatry, pathology, bacteriology, and many others. Although they were not known by these names in Hippocrates' time, he made vital contributions to many of them. Let us look into Hippocrates' own records and see what advances he introduced as he converted medicine into a science.

Physiology

Physiology is the science dealing with the functions of various organs of the body. In one of Hippocrates' writings, called *Airs, Waters and Places,* he described the effect that climate can have on the habits of life, especially on eating and drinking. Hippocrates wrote much on the explanation of digestion—the breakdown of foods in the body. He said that special body fluids were involved. Today we call these fluids *digestive enzymes*. Although he didn't know it at the time, Hippocrates contributed to the knowledge of the physiology of digestion.

Physical Diagnosis

Physical diagnosis is the determination of disease by external examination of the body. Hippocrates was a great believer in this practice, as are all medical men today. His entire theory of medicine was based upon close attention to observation, and he constantly advised Greek physicians to observe their patients meticulously. He told them to look at the eyes, the skin, the ears, and the forehead; to listen to the chest, the heartbeat, and the lungs for signs of disease. Indeed, nothing was more characteristic of Hippocratic medicine than this insistence on the closest attention to the patient. Here is his advice to contemporary colleagues:

One must note the following: conditions that disappear of their own accord; blisters such as come from fire, where this or that is beneficial or harmful; shapes of parts affected, kinds of motion, swelling, subsidence of swelling, sleep, wakefulness, restlessness, yawning;—lose no time in acting or preventing; vomit, evacuations, spittle, mucus, coughing, belching, swallowing, hiccup, flatulence, urine, sneezing, tears, scratching, plucking or feeling (at hairs or bedding), thirst, hunger, plethora, dreams, pain, absence of pain, the body, the mind, ability to take in one's meaning, memory, voice, persistent silence.

Hippocrates also had his students learn the technique of taking down a medical history; that is, asking questions of the patient to learn about sleep habits, nature of employment, exposure to others who were ill, and the like. Today, a physician combines the methods of physical diagnosis and medical history to inform himself of a patient's problems and needs.

Pathology

Pathology is the scientific study of the changes in the body produced by disease. Hippocrates recognized early that a physician must develop a clear idea of normal bodily structure and function so as to determine what is abnormal and diseased.

Hippocrates made many contributions to pathology.

Among them were his work on the influence of diet on disease, his study of how disease spread from person to person, and the importance of body fluids to disease. He also felt that the good or bad quality of the blood was a very good indicator of disease. Today pathologists do a great deal of examination of blood specimens for signs of disease.

Surgery

Surgery is that branch of medicine which treats disease by manual and operative procedures. Hippocrates taught his students and future physicians the methods and techniques of surgery. He stressed the importance of a surgeon's having a good assistant and correct instruments. As long as two thousand years ago, Hippocrates realized the importance to a surgeon of direct lighting. In his writings on *The Art of Medicine*, he describes how to put silk over the light to diffuse it and eliminate shadows. That Hippocrates was capable of understanding and pioneering these basic medical and surgical principles before anyone else is indisputable proof of his genius.

Moreover, Hippocrates felt that one of the important techniques a physician should learn early is how to bandage. This illustrates Hippocrates' basic concern for details, for it is known that he spent considerable time teaching his students proper bandaging methods.

Fever

Fever is a symptom of disease that results in increased body temperature, and Hippocrates recognized it as the most important single sign of disease. He also noticed that some fevers were of an epidemic nature, that is, they occurred among a very large number of people at the same time. He further discovered that fever can occur in a single isolated individual without spreading to others. Hippocrates taught his medical students to follow this symptom closely, and to study its effect on the patient along with observation of the patient's breathing and perspiring. In addition, he told them that a fever which progressed rapidly was the most dangerous. Hippocrates even knew that some fevers would disappear suddenly, and he tried to formulate generalities about fevers as an aid in predicting the outcome of disease.

In this way, Hippocrates contributed to *microbiology,* the branch of medicine which deals with microbes such as bacteria and viruses. These microscopic organisms often cause infections in man and usually the first sign of such an infection is a fever.

Neurology and Psychiatry

Neurology and *psychiatry* are branches of medicine which are concerned with diseases and disorders of the nervous system. Neurology usually deals with nerve disease; psychiatry with emotional problems of the mind.

Hippocrates' intimate knowledge of the function of the human brain led him to his contributions to these fields. He said that men ought to know that from the brain, and from the brain only, arise our pleasures, joys, laughter, and jests, as well as our sorrows, pains, griefs, and tears. Through it, in particular, we think, see, hear, and distinguish the ugly from the beautiful, the bad from the good, the pleasant from the unpleasant.

Moreover, said Hippocrates, the brain is the most powerful organ of the human body, for when it is healthy it interprets the phenomena surrounding us. Eyes, ears, tongue, hands, and feet act in accordance with the discernment of the brain; in fact, the whole body participates in intelligence in proportion to the brain's activity.

The writings of Hippocrates also state that the brain is to be looked upon as the seat of the intellect and that, in conditions of increased or decreased warmth or humidity, disease symptoms occur. Temporary fears, terrors, and deliria are due to damage to the brain. Temporary depressions are due also to disorders of the brain, according to Hippocrates.

There was one disease prevalent during Hippocrates' time which many people believed was caused by demons and gods; it was called, therefore, the "Sacred Disease." Hippocrates said of this disease, however, that it was no more divine or sacred than any other disease. On the contrary, the great physician maintained, it had specific characteristics and a definite cause. Yet, because it was so completely different from other diseases, it had always been regarded with ignorance and astonishment. Hippocrates had this to say about it:

It is my opinion that those who first called this disease "sacred" were the sort of people we now call witch-doctors, faith-healers, quacks and charlatans. By invoking a divine element they were able to screen their own failure to give treatment and so called this a "sacred" illness to conceal their ignorance of its nature by picking their phrases carefully, prescribing purifications and magic along with many foods which were really unsuitable for the sick.

Whatever this disease was—it may have been a type of mental illness; we do not know today—Hippocrates believed that it was hereditary. Further, he suspected that the brain was the seat of the disease, as it was of other very violent diseases.

Pharmacology

Pharmacology is the study of drugs, their sources, and their use. Our terms pharmacology, pharmacy, and pharmaceutical are derived from the Greek word *pharmakon* which the Greek poet, Homer, used to mean "drug."

Early Greek therapy involved the use of transplanted Egyptian plant medicines, modified by beliefs of a magical nature. The Rx with which the modern physician begins his prescriptions is a sign that has its origins in the ancient pagan symbol for Jupiter, and was originally written as an invocation to that god.

With the growth of temple medicine, the physicians at the Asclepieia, in an effort to increase the reputations of their own particular temples, introduced more and more drugs. In his time, Hippocrates reacted against this mass of uncertain knowledge about drugs and, although the followers of Hippocrates were familiar with the properties of a great many of them, they usually confined therapy to practical, corrective measures. Moreover, Hippocrates' followers placed considerable emphasis upon the proper types of food and advised a well-balanced diet. It was also not unusual for them to order the removal of a patient to a better climate or to prescribe massage and baths to relieve his sufferings.

One favorite dietetic remedy of Hippocrates was honey boiled in water, and he gave specific directions for its preparation:

Hydromel, increases thirst less than sweet wine; it softens the lungs, is moderately expectorant, and alleviates a cough; for it has some detergent quality in it, whence it lubricates the sputum. Hydromel is also moderately diuretic. ——Boiled hydromel has a much more elegant appearance than the unboiled, being clear, thin, white and transparent, but I am unable to mention any good quality which it possesses that the other wants. For it is not sweeter than the unboiled, provided the honey be fine. But one should by all means use it boiled, provided the honey be bad, impure, black and not fragrant, for the boiling will remove the most of its bad qualities and appearances.

Oxymel (honey in vinegar) was also employed by Hippocrates in the treatment of acute diseases:

Oxymel promotes expectoration and freedom of breathing. It also promotes flatulent discharges from the bowels, and is diuretic.

The universal laxative of that period was a plant called hellebore. It is apparent that Hippocrates and his followers employed this drug with caution, for practitioners were admonished to be wary of its use:

Hellebore is dangerous to persons whose flesh is sound, for it induces convulsions. When you wish the hellebore to act more, move the body, and when to stop, let the patient get sleep and rest. A spasm from taking hellebore is of a fatal nature.

Thus, it is evident that Hippocrates did not believe in magical remedies. Indeed, Hippocrates continually emphasized that disease is not produced by the gods. Rather, he remained convinced that all illness must have a specific, human cause, and that by employing practical, scientific methods it could be successfully treated.

SEVEN

Hippocrates as a Physician

The personal impact of Hippocrates on the community of Cos was great indeed. To have such a physician practicing in their midst made the people of the island extremely proud. In fact, Cos became well known throughout the Greek world because the great teacher of medicine worked and taught there. Hippocrates' days were filled with much activity. He had numerous duties to perform in teaching his students and followers. In addition, his services became so popular that almost every ill person wished to be treated by him.

Hippocrates obviously believed that "learning by doing" was a valuable method of teaching. He continually used his students as assistants during his medical practice and visits to patients. Most often, however, his patients came to him; then Hippocrates had a better chance to teach more students important things by letting them look on.

In some of his writings, Hippocrates left records of his patients—their names, their illnesses, occasionally his method of treatment, and the final results. These case histories, together with some of Hippocrates' lecture notes from his writings on *The Art of Medicine* enable us to follow a typical day of medical care and teaching carried out by Hippocrates.

Early in the morning, Hippocrates visited those patients who were bedridden, either in their homes or in his healing temple. This gave him an opportunity to learn whether they had had a restful night and how much progress they were making. This procedure parallels that of a modern physician who visits his hospitalized patients in the morning before beginning his regular office hours.

From his own records, Hippocrates tells us that on one typical day he went to see a man named Philiseus who was in bed with a high fever. The description of the fever sounds much like malaria. Hippocrates did what he could to make his patient comfortable, but there was no drug to use for this disease in those days, and we have to assume that this patient was not cured.

Hippocrates next went to visit Herephon, a young man of Cos who had had a fever for seventeen days; finally, following treatment by Hippocrates, the fever broke on the eighteenth day and Herephon became well again.

Another patient visited by Hippocrates was the daughter of his friend Pausanias. She had foolishly eaten raw mushrooms and had become violently ill. Hippocrates gave her warm honey and other medicants to cause her to bring up the bad food, and in a few hours she was well.

Another case reported by Hippocrates tells of his visiting the house of Ariston, a sculptor of Cos, and finding a very sick woman. She had a sore, red throat and a high fever. This sounds much like tonsillitis, and the modern doctor would use penicillin; instead, Hippocrates had to use a poultice, or hot pack, to cure this patient.

In his day-to-day caring for the sick people of Cos, Hippocrates often had to treat those who were mentally ill. He relates one successful encounter with a woman who was so grief-stricken over the loss of her husband that she refused to eat or sleep. As a result she lost weight and became ill; her children called on Hippocrates for help. First, Hippocrates let her tell of her grief and sadness. Then he counseled her, explained how her behavior was affecting her entire family, and how she was, in turn, bringing grief to them. By pointing out to the woman her children's need and dependence on her, he was able to bring her out of her state of despondency. In this instance Hippocrates—although he did not know it—was practicing what today we term psychiatry.

After spending the early part of the day visiting patients at home and receiving them at the temple, Hippocrates would eat his midday meal and prepare to meet his new medical students. When he did so, Hippocrates usually lectured them on the meaning of medicine and the importance of patient care. From his works on *The Art of Medicine, Airs, Waters, and Places,* and *Regimen in Acute Diseases and Aphorisms,* we can easily reconstruct such a lecture in Hippocrates' own words:

"Whoever wishes to pursue properly the science of medicine must have natural ability and good teaching. I would define medicine as the removal of two classes of illness from the sick. There is the group in which all symptoms can be seen by the eye or touched by the hand. These are called the external diseases. There are other diseases, most numerous, called internal diseases, which include diseases of the bones and organs, and these cannot be seen by the eye. The symptoms which patients with internal diseases describe to their physician are, unfortunately, only guesses. Thus the science of medicine is demonstrated when it can relieve an internal disease. This is what you young students must master as you study and work to learn the science of medicine. Heal the internal diseases.

"One of the first rules a young physician should learn is that nursing care is important to the relief of illness.

"The room in which the sick person lies should be shaded, comfortable and not exposed to the winds. Preferably it should be darkened; not in the upper floor; there should not be too many visitors and there should be little walking around. The patient too should remain quiet and not talk. He should not twist around and should not get up, apart from the toilet; he should not expose the body to chill, and thereby increase the fever. Clothing and covers should be soft and clean.

"Do not do anything that causes violent exertion; too much of anything is always harmful, but give large quantities of drinks. Bowel movements can be provided by giving proper diet or mild enemas. At all times proper ventilation should be favored.

"It is also very important for a physician to be able to tell his patients not only about their past and present symptoms but also about what is going to occur; this is prognosis. By prolonged study and observation of

73

many patients and disease conditions seen all over the Greek world, I have accumulated information which will aid in prognosis. Some of these bits of information, called *aphorisms,* I shall give you now, but there are many more and they all must be learned before you become effective physicians:

"In acute disease it is not quite safe to predict either death or recovery.

"Persons who are naturally very fat are apt to die earlier than those who are slender.

"In old people it is common to find coughs, pains of the joints, dimness of sign, cataract, glaucoma, and dullness of hearing.

"It is bad when slight sweating and sleeplessness are followed by a rise in temperature.

"Slight sweating in a fever is a bad sign.

"To jump on being touched, is bad.

"In acute fevers it is bad to be chilled externally but to burn inside and to be thirsty.

"Fourteen days mark the crisis in fever of the acute type, bringing either alleviation or death.

"Acute diseases reach a crisis in fourteen days.

"Undisturbed sleep denotes a safe crisis; disturbed sleep with bodily pain, an unsure one.

"Drowsiness is altogether bad.

"Buzzing and noises in the ears is a bad sign in acute disease.

"A shaggy, very dry tongue is a sign of brain-fever.

"Frequent attacks of pain in the heart in an old person often denote sudden death."

In all, Hippocrates wrote more than six hundred aphorisms. They served as guides to prognosis to enable the physician to predict the course of disease. Some of them have become part of the weapons a modern doctor uses in fighting sickness.

Thus, Hippocrates' contributions both as physician

and teacher were numerous. As a result of his wide influence on the Greek world, many honors were bestowed upon him. Statues were erected in his honor, some in Cos and others all over Greece. Today, several museums in Rome have statues or busts of Hippocrates. The greatest honor, however, was bestowed upon Hippocrates by his students and followers. These men thought so much of their master that they signed his name to their own medical works, feeling that all their knowledge came from him. Thus, as we shall see, medical works written by many other physicians have come down through the ages signed "Hippocrates."

The Men Who Followed

Through the ages, since Hippocrates' time, there have been handed down from generation to generation some seventy-six works of medical reference, all signed with the name "Hippocrates" and called *The Hippocratic Corpus,* or "Hippocratic Collection."

However, since we know that Hippocrates himself was named for his grandfather and that it was common for names to be used again and again in Greek families, the question arises: Were all these medical works written by one man? If not, which men were those who followed the Father of Medicine in recording their valuable observations and ideas under Hippocrates' name?

After careful study and research, scholars today feel that most of these works which we credit to the Father of Medicine stemmed directly from him or from his students and followers. Indeed, many of Hippocrates' sons and grandsons who followed in their famous relative's footsteps, showed their allegiance by signing their own works with his name. These men are often called the "disciples" of Hippocrates.

In fact, Hippocrates' two sons, Thessalus and Draco, were themselves physicians and carried on the medical tradition of their celebrated father. Draco became physician to the King of Macedonia, and Thessalus was also a physician to royalty. These two, plus Apollonius, Polybus, and Dexippus, pupils of Hippocrates, were important men who spread the master's word throughout the Greek world and beyond. One of the three, Polybus, was a son-in-law of Hippocrates and wrote many works in physiology and anatomy and named his own son Hippocrates III.

Perhaps one of the most brilliant of Hippocrates' disciples was Diocles, himself a nephew of the Father of Medicine. Diocles was regarded as the greatest physician, next to Hippocrates, and he made many contributions to medicine. He wrote books on drugs and poisons, and looked upon the heart as the center of the body and source of blood. He also emphasized practical experience and bedside observation. A faithful follower of Hippocrates, he was highly thought of by his colleagues. At least three medical works of Diocles are signed with Hippocrates' name.

As a follower of Diocles, the next physician of importance was Praxagoras of Cos who lived about 330 B.C. His chief contribution to medicine was that he made a distinction between arteries and veins, although he made the mistake of thinking only veins contained blood. It was many years before this error was corrected. Another important contribution of Praxagoras was that he revealed the importance of the pulse in making a medical diagnosis. He is also credited with being among the first to study anatomy by human dissection.

From all available records, it appears that Hippocrates probably died at the age of ninety-nine in 361 B.C. After his death, the science of medicine suffered a setback. Although his followers tried to maintain the high standards which Hippocrates had set, they were far from being the genius he had been. Thus, due to their increasingly ineffectual methods, Greek medicine declined. It was during this period that the world center of medicine shifted from Greece to Egypt—which meant from Cos and Athens across the Mediterranean to Alexandria. The Greeks did not recover the lead in medicine until the time of Galen, several hundred years later. Also, during the years following Hippocrates' death, the centers of culture and learning—the museums, libraries, and medical schools—began to appear in Alexandria.

One of the doctors who contributed to the reputation of the Alexandrian medical center was Herophilus, a pupil of Praxagoras. In a way, he too was of the Hippocratic school, since he was a pupil of a pupil of the great master. Herophilus made many great contributions to anatomy which today are still accepted as valid. Attracting many students from all over the world, he was the first to study the anatomy of the brain and the spinal cord, and to show that the brain was the center of intelligence. This physician traced the nerves from brain to spine; described the optic nerve and blood vessels; studied and wrote about pulse rate, the liver, pancreas, and other parts of the human body never before accurately reported. His contributions were very numerous and valuable to later physicians.

A few years later, there appeared in Alexandria another physician of importance named Erasistratus. He made careful studies of the brain, and of the heart and its valves. He named the trachea (windpipe) and described the spleen, kidneys, and intestines. Erasistratus spent many years in travel and research. He mastered the Hippocratic writings and visited the famous physicians and surgeons of his time. For a time he was a court physician to a king.

While the contributions to medicine made by these men were important, no individual doctor came close to achieving the stature of Hippocrates for at least six hundred years following his death. It was only in the second century of the Christian era that another such renowned physician came on the scene. This man was named Claudius Galenus, who is known to history simply as "Galen."

Galen was born in the year 130 A.D. in the city of Pergamos in Greece. His father Nicon, a distinguished architect, saw to it that his son had a good education in mathematics, literature, and philosophy. However, when Galen was seventeen, his father dreamed that he saw Asclepius who told him that his son should become a physician. Thus, in the year 147 A.D., Galen left Pergamos for Smyrna, another part of Greece, to learn medicine. Later, Galen traveled extensively in order to perfect his education. For approximately ten years, he wandered through Palestine and Asia Minor, finally coming to Alexandria, which still retained some of the ancient fame it had enjoyed during the days of Herophilus and Erasistratus. In Alexandria, Galen wrote medical works on anatomy and physiology and soon acquired stature as a physician. On his return to Pergamos, at the age of twenty-eight, Galen was appointed physician to the gladiators, those fierce fighters who battled each other for the entertainment of the public. This provided him with excellent practical experience in anatomy and surgery. Indeed, Galen did such an excellent job of patching up these battered warriors that he came to be called *Paradoxopoeus*—"The Wonder Worker." He also wrote further works at this time, one of which was called *Diagnosis of Diseases of the Eye.*

Galen remained as physician to the gladiators for four years, and then traveled to Rome where he took up his own medical practice. He soon gained a wide reputation as a great physician, and men of great importance came to him for diagnosis and treatment. All during his practice, however, he studied and wrote, gave teaching demonstrations, and promoted the medicine of Hippocrates among his colleagues. Galen was an avid follower of Hippocratic medicine and always referred to Hippocrates in worshipful and praiseworthy terms. He felt that he, himself, was the successor to Hippocrates.

Ultimately, Galen became the court physician to the Roman Emperor, Marcus Aurelius. He held this position from 169–180 A.D. During this time he produced his most extensive writings—works which dominated the world of medicine for the next fourteen hundred years! He worked long and hard until the day of his death, which is said to have occurred in 201 A.D. in Sicily.

Galen was a prolific writer, indeed. He wrote some five hundred works on philosophy and medicine in clear Greek. Unfortunately, most of his works were lost to western Europe after the break-up of the Roman Empire. However, more than one hundred have survived, and from them we can gain a good insight into Galen's contributions to medicine.

His anatomical investigations were unrivaled in antiquity for their completeness and accuracy. Galen dissected apes and lower animals, although much that is relevant to the human body is also incorporated in his works. His physiological investigations were revolutionary. One of his greatest contributions was the demonstration that the arteries contain blood, and not air, as the Alexandrian school had taught for over four hundred years.

Galen's teachings on fractures and dislocations showed many advances over those of Hippocrates. He was the first to discover that one could obtain useful drugs by chemically extracting them from plants. In fact, Galen thought so much of his own ability to treat disease that in one of his own books he said, "No one before me has given the true method of treating disease. Hippocrates has opened the path but left for a successor to enlarge and make it plain." Here, obviously, was a man who thought quite highly of himself! And, indeed, there was scarcely a subject in medicine which was not covered by Galen's genius.

Hippocrates and Galen were the two greatest physicians in the history of ancient medicine. Although, ultimately, some of Galen's work was discredited, the total value of it cannot be overlooked. Galen was the last of the Greeks to hold up the banner of medical science. With his death, creativity in medicine slumbered for many, many years.

NINE

Hippocrates and a Guide to Modern Health

Among the many writings and records left by Hippocrates was one called *A Regimen for Health*. This was essentially a guide for the people of the day containing advice on how to keep well. In it, Hippocrates wrote about subjects such as exercise, food, diet; and also about the care of the teeth, skin, and the body in general.

If we examine some of Hippocrates' suggestions and compare them with what we do today to keep healthy we will see how he has influenced modern rules of good health.

Exercise

Hippocrates felt that exercises such as running and wrestling were important in maintaining good health. Warning his readers against exercising too long and becoming exhausted, he advised frequent rest periods.

Hippocrates also felt that exercise should not be done immediately after eating since it interfered with proper digestion of food. How does all this compare with modern ideas of exercise and rest?

Today we recognize that exercise is necessary for good health. If a moderate amount of exercise is not performed, muscles lose strength, become flabby, and are easily subject to injury. Moreover, it is known that proper balance of exercise and rest is required; and that overexertion or too much exercise, especially in older people, is as bad as no exercise at all. On the other hand, young people usually are capable of more spirited activity and can engage in tennis, handball, and football without harm. Less strenuous kinds of recreational exercise such as golf, swimming, and walking are best for older persons.

Thus, it can be seen that Hippocrates' recommendations have been followed by succeeding generations, and moderate exercise remains one of the keys to good health.

Diet

It is well recognized today that the diet of an individual influences his health. Hippocrates knew this well and said that the food people ate should depend upon their age, their habits, their work, and the time of year. He wrote that soft, moist foods are best in early life (infants) and during illness because they are easily digested. Hippocrates also advised people to eat less during summer months and more during winter. He gave advice to obese people on how to keep their weight down. Hippocrates in some way knew that foods were more healthful when boiled and baked, rather than fried. Indeed, he followed this advice himself and recommended it to his followers.

In his writings, Hippocrates was also careful to describe those foods which he felt were most important for growth and development. He mentioned fruits, vegetables, the meat from animals that feed on grass, milk, and cereals. Hippocrates also felt that wine was good for the body, but for adults, of course, and not children. True, we know today that Hippocrates did not know about vitamins and other chemicals inherent in foods which are important to the life process, but he must have seen how his patients thrived on proper foods!

In fact, today's guide for necessary foods is almost exactly the same as that proposed by Hippocrates two thousand years ago. We know this group as the "basic seven" foods. It includes: (1) green and yellow vegetables, (2) citrus fruits, (3) potatoes, (4) milk, (5) meats, (6) bread and cereals, and (7) butter or margarine. Of this "basic seven," Hippocrates failed to mention only one or two in his writings.

What Hippocrates could not know, of course, were the names of the vital chemicals within these foods—chemicals that all of us need in order to live. Milk provides many important minerals but calcium, which is needed for bone formation, is the most important. Meats provide protein—the "building blocks" for muscle and tissue. Fruits and vegetables furnish vitamins and minerals, which help the human body to use its food to build good health. Finally, bread and cereals provide the energy we need for daily activities.

Still, even though Hippocrates did not possess this modern chemical knowledge, he knew his foods well and realized how much they could contribute toward a longer, healthier life.

The Skin

The outer covering of the body, Hippocrates wrote, consists of skin and its branches, the hair and nails. All of these have very important functions. They protect the organs and tissues from injury, keep out infectious germs, regulate the body temperature, and aid in the elimination of bodily wastes through perspiration.

Hippocrates made many recommendations concerning skin care. Not only did he advise that a bath should be taken every day, he even described in exact detail how warm the water should be, how important it was to prevent chills, and how useful a sponge was for proper cleansing. Moreover, Hippocrates taught that regular bathing in warm water had the effect of soothing mild pain, relieving fatigue, softening the skin, and washing away waste products of the body.

Hippocrates knew of diseases of the skin such as warts and acne. He recognized that they occurred frequently in children and in young adults. He recommended a well-balanced diet, adequate sleep, and cleanliness for the treatment of acne, but wisely said nothing about wart treatment. Today we know that warts are caused by a specific virus or tiny microbe, and they must be removed only under the strict care of a physician.

The Teeth

Hippocrates correctly described the formation, care, and diseases of the teeth. He revealed to his students that infants have fever and mild illness when they are cutting teeth, but that this is only temporary and natural. Hippocrates also taught his medical students that although some animals are born with teeth, children do not begin to cut their teeth until many months after birth. In addition, he explained that diseases of the teeth—especially tooth decay—were often related to the type of diet an individual followed.

And today there is general agreement that diet— just as Hippocrates taught—is the most important single factor in the maintenance of sound teeth. This is particularly true during the period of growth from infancy through childhood; carbohydrates, which make up most of the food material in candies, chocolate, gum, and other sugar foods, are especially harmful in excessive quantities. Many dentists feel that *caries,* or decay of the teeth, come from the chemical action of bacteria in the mouth working on carbohydrate foodstuffs between and on the teeth. Of course, Hippocrates did not know of this in his day, but he did correctly observe that proper diet resulted in healthy teeth.

The Eyes

Hippocrates treated and wrote about more than twenty disease conditions of the eyes. He taught his followers all he knew about symptoms of eye disease, care of the eyes, the significance of squinting and other abnormalities of the eye. Most of this information is available today in a document by Hippocrates called *On the Power of Vision.* In it, Hippocrates taught that the eye is one of the most important organs of the body. He wrote that the greatest amount of information is acquired by vision, followed by hearing, smelling, tasting, and touching. This is true because the eye behaves in such a way as to record what it sees in the mind.

In addition, Hippocrates explained that the condition of the eyes could reveal to the physician the general health of a patient. He advised his students to examine the eyes carefully, to look for swellings, sensitivity to light, inflammation, tearing, and continuous blinking. He also knew that headaches could be associated with eye disorders as well as complaints in other parts of the human body. He further taught that pains in the eyes were to be investigated closely because they often indicated serious illness.

Although Hippocrates was able to contribute a great deal to our knowledge of the eye and its diseases, he naturally did not have available to him the modern instruments and equipment for accurately studying that organ. As a result of modern advances, we have been able to formulate guides to care of the eyes and prevention of eyestrain. Such modern advances as eye exercises, eye specialists, studies of illumination, and scientific instrumentation have served to provide improved care of vision.

Yet even in his own day, Hippocrates realized that eyes can stand considerable abuse; however, he also realized that if one expected efficient service from them day after day and year after year, they should be given reasonable care. When used for close work, for example, the eyes should be rested at frequent intervals. And, during illness and convalescence, they are susceptible to fatigue and so should be used sparingly.

Moreover, Hippocrates emphasized again and again, it is important to realize that the condition of the eye and the general health are closely related. Poor vision may be due to a specific disease or may be aggravated by poor general health, and eyestrain may give rise to symptoms in other parts of the body. When the eye is involved, the best care and treatment are needed because the possibility of preventing loss of vision may depend upon early recognition and proper treatment of disease of the eye.

The Hippocratic Oath and the Modern Physician

Among all the noteworthy contributions that Hippocrates made to medicine, none is more highly regarded than the *Hippocratic Oath*. Actually, it is doubtful whether Hippocrates himself wrote this oath. Rather, it would seem that the Hippocratic Oath is an outgrowth of Hippocrates' own inspired ideals by which a physician ought to practice medicine.

From the written records of Hippocrates' activities, we can easily find examples of these ideas which eventually became incorporated into the oath. For example, Hippocrates said, "An Asclepiad who is summoned to treat the sick at the home should never mention outside the house those things which the master of the house does not want known." This same idea is incorporated in the oath that has been handed down through history.

On another occasion, Hippocrates was asked for poison by one of his patients, Empedocles, who had a long-term illness. Hippocrates said that it was the task of the physician to save life, not to end it. Again, Hippocrates advised that every physician should ask for medical advice from his fellows. "At all times he should make no effort to dazzle the patient; give no lectures for the purpose of increasing his reputation; make no pretense to infallibility; have regard to personal cleanliness; use elegance without luxury and perfumes with restraint."

All of these teachings and ideals of Hippocrates finally took the form of an oath which physicians adopted during the fourth century B.C. The Hippocratic Oath, in part, is this:

I swear by Apollo, the Physician, by Asclepius, Hygieia, Panaceia, and all the gods and goddesses . . . that I will carry out, according to the best of my ability and judgment, this oath and covenant: . . . I will, according to my ability and judgment, prescribe such treatment for my patients as may be most beneficial to them, seeking to keep from them anything that may prove to be wrong or injurious . . . I will maintain the purity and integrity of both my life and my profession . . . Into whatever houses I enter, I will go there for the benefit of the sick; I will abstain from all intentional wrongdoing and harm, especially from abusing the body of man or woman, bond or free.

If in the practice of my profession—or in social life outside of it—I chance to see or hear anything that should not be told abroad, I will hold it a secret and maintain on that subject a religious silence. If, therefore, I conscientiously observe this my oath and do not break it, may it be mine to enjoy in the eyes of all men a good reputation for the manner of my life and the practice of my profession; but if I break my oath or transgress it, may the opposite be my lot.

Primarily a pronouncement of medical ethics, the Hippocratic Oath itself is not a set of laws enforced upon the physician by an authority; rather, it is a guide which he accepts of his own free will. Indeed, far from being a legal document it is, as the wording indicates, a solemn promise given by the conscience of the physician who swears to it. This again is in keeping with Hippocratic medicine, for the great teacher insisted that all instruction must be based on the willingness of teacher and pupil—on voluntary rules as well as voluntary obedience.

Today this oath is sworn to by medical graduates on

the day they receive their degrees as Doctor of Medicine. Let us examine some of the more important parts of the oath and see how the modern physician follows its preachings.

I swear by Apollo, the Physician, by Asclepius, Hygieia, Panaceia, and all the gods and goddesses . . .

Who are these figures that are mentioned in the opening of the Hippocratic Oath? During classical Greek times, Apollo was the god of the sun, light, and air. He was also thought of as the father of Asclepius, the legendary physician who was the figurehead of the Asclepiads, the group of physicians from which Hippocrates descended. Hygieia means health and Panaceia means "all healing." So we see that the introductory words to the Oath of Hippocrates are spoken before the mythical gods of health and healing. Thus, when all new physicians take this oath, the words go back two thousand years in history.

. . . that I will carry out, according to the best of my ability and judgment, this oath . . .

With these words the modern physician promises to do his best to follow the oath. He doesn't try to do the impossible, because the oath says, "to the best of my ability." And, further:

I will, according to my ability and judgment, prescribe such treatment for my patients as may be most beneficial to them, seeking to keep them from anything that may prove to be wrong or injurious . . .

This part of the oath is followed very closely by today's doctors. They treat according to their ability. This means that sometimes a family doctor recognizes that some patients require a physician especially trained to treat certain diseases. The family doctor does whatever he can for his patient, then calls in a *specialist*. In addition, the physician of today will not give harmful or injurious drugs as was done in former times. His oath forbids it. The oath goes on:

I will maintain the purity and integrity of both my life and my profession . . .

Here the physician of today—as in years gone by— promises that he will not bring any shame or harm to his profession and that he will, as well, lead a pure and noble life. In this way he can help keep the profession of medicine on a high level and bring respect to his fellow physicians.

Into whatever houses I enter, I will go there for the benefit of the sick . . .

How often have you seen the physician with his little black bag enter a house? He is going for the benefit of the sick; he is following his sworn oath and entering with the hope of improving the condition of the ill and reducing their suffering.

If in the practice of my profession . . . I chance to see or hear anything that should not be told abroad, I will hold it a secret . . .

This is a very strict rule of the physician. He never tells anyone the things that his patients want kept secret. In this he is like a minister or a rabbi. A doctor-patient relationship is a bond between those two and no one can break it. This means that you can always confide in your doctor; he has promised to keep your confidence.

As this account of the emergence of scientific medicine closes, one fact stands out clearly: we have encountered a man of genius who fathered the science of medicine and left his imprint to be felt two thousand years after his death. He was a man who based his reasoning on his own observation—a man who found a way to assist the body in its fight against disease. Indeed, his own meticulous writings show that he set broken bones, carried out operations, and treated all illnesses to the best of his ability. He had clear vision, great knowledge, and stood for honesty and accuracy in all things. This was Hippocrates.

Index

A

Academy, Athens, 27
Acute diseases, 32, 66
Acute Diseases, Regimen in, Hippocrates, 72
Aegean islands, 9–10, 11
Aegean Sea, 5, 6, 8
Aeolians, 12, 14–15
Airs, Waters and Places, Hippocrates, 57, 72
Alexandria, center of medical science, 79–80, 81
Amputations, in prehistorical times, 46–47
Anatomy:
   Galen's study of, 83
   Herophilus' contributions to, 80
   study by human dissection, 79
Aphorisms, Hippocrates, 72, 74–75
Apollo, god, 38, 96
Apollonius, pupil of Hippocrates, 78
Art of Medicine, The, Hippocrates, 60, 70, 72
Arteries. *See* Circulatory system
Artists' profession in ancient Greece, 37–38

Asclepiads, priest-physicians, 29, 30, 53, 55, 96
Asclepieions, temples of Asclepius, 29, 40, 53–55
Asclepius, 29, 30, 40, 53, 96
Assistants, medical, in ancient Greece, 40, 41
Athenian citizens, 13
Athens, 13, 29
   gymnasiums of, 27
   health and hygiene in, 39, 41
Authorship of works signed "Hippocrates," 17, 76, 77–78

B

Bandaging methods, 61
Barbers, in ancient Greece, 43
Blood vessels and circulation. *See* circulatory system
Booksellers in ancient Greece, 37
Brain:
   Herophilus' study of, 80
   Hippocrates' knowledge of, 62–64
   progress in understanding of, after Hippocrates, 80

C

Carpathos (Karpathos), island of, 11

Case histories, Hippocrates', 70

Chinese medicine, 49–51

Chios, island of, 10

Circulatory system (heart, arteries, veins), growing understanding of, 78, 79, 80, 83

Cnidian Maxims, Euryphon, 31

Cnidus, island of, medical school on, 30, 31, 32

Coans, adherents of the Cos medical school, 31–32

Corcyra (Corfu), island of, 9

Cos, Island of, 1, 11–12, 69, 76, 79 medical school on, 30, 31, 32

Crafts and trades in Hippocrates' day, 42–44

Crete, island of, 10–11, 13

D

Democritus, 1

Dentistry, in ancient Greece, 40

Dexippus, pupil of Hippocrates, 78

Diagnosis. *See* Physical diagnosis

Diagnosis of Diseases of the Eye, Galen, 82

Diet, 86, 87–88 Hippocrates' views on, 65, 86–87, 90

Digestion, physiology of, 57–58

Diocles, pupil of Hippocrates, 78

Disease: acute, 32, 66 in Biblical times, 52 epidemics, 39, 41, 50, 52, 60 Hippocrates on nature and cause of, 2, 67 Plato on, 41 "Sacred," and Hippocrates' opinion, 63–64 *See also* Treatment

Dissection, study of anatomy by, 79

Doctors. *See* Physicians

Doctors' offices in ancient Greece, 40

Dorians, 12–13

Draco, son of Hippocrates, 78

Drugs: dispensing, in Hippocrates' time, 40, 41 Egyptian, 48, 64 Greek Asclepian, 54, 64–65 hypnotic, 54 Hippocrates' use of, 65–66 progress after Hippocrates, 78, 83

Dysentery, 52

E

Ebers Papyrus, 48–49

Egyptian medicine, 47–49 influence on Greek medicine, 31, 32, 64

Epidemics, 39, 41 in ancient Israel, 52 Hippocrates' study of, 60

THE AUTHOR

HERBERT S. GOLDBERG was born
in New York City and is a profes-
sor of microbiology at the Uni-
versity of Missouri. He has long
been interested in bringing knowledge of biology and medicine to
the public. He has accomplished
this by writing on a variety of
medical subjects, as well as lectur-
ing on them in this country and
abroad.

978-0-595-38023-7
0-595-38023-9

Printed in the United States
45176LVS00002B/37-66

9 780595 380237